Let's Talk About

BEING DESTRUCTIVE

Distributed by:

Word, Incorporated
4800 W. Waco Drive
Waco, TX 76703

Let's Talk About

BEING DESTRUCTIVE

By JOY BERRY

Illustrated by John Costanza
Edited by Orly Kelly
Designed by Jill Losson

Living Skills Press
Fallbrook, California

Let's talk about BEING DESTRUCTIVE.

When you damage something or destroy it, you are BEING DESTRUCTIVE.

Breaking something is being destructive.

When you break other people's things, you should do everything you can to fix them. If you cannot fix them yourself, you should try to get someone to fix them for you.

Ruining something is being destructive.

When you ruin other people's things, you should do everything you can to replace them.

Making a mess is being destructive.

When you make a mess, you should clean it up.

Your *curiosity* may cause you to be destructive.

When you are curious, you want to learn about things that are new, strange, or interesting. You might handle something so that you can learn about it. If you do not know how to handle something the right way, you may break or ruin it.

To make sure that this does not happen, you need to ask questions. Find out what something is and how it works *before* you handle it.

You may *accidentally* be destructive. Without meaning to, you might break or ruin something.

Be careful so that this will not happen often. Pay attention to what you are doing. Handle things carefully. Move carefully when you are around things that are easily broken.

Your *carelessness* may cause you to be destructive. When you do not care about something, you might break or ruin it.

You need to care about the things around you. Realize that they are important, and take care of them.

Your *anger* or *frustration* may cause you to be destructive. When you get angry or frustrated you may want to hit, kick, throw, or smash something. The thing you abuse may get broken or be ruined.

Do not handle anything that could get damaged or be destroyed when you are angry or frustrated. Wait until you calm down.

Someone might tell you that you may not go into an area. This may happen because the area has things in it that can be broken or ruined. It may also happen because the person does not think that you will be careful.

Do not go into areas that you have been told to stay out of.

Someone might tell you that you may not touch certain things. This may happen because the things can be broken or ruined. It may also happen because the person does not think that you will be careful.

Do not touch things that you are not supposed to touch.

If you *disobey* and are destructive, you may
need to be punished.

Hopefully the punishment will help you to learn
that you need to obey when you are asked
to leave something alone.

If you are destructive because you *do not care,* you may need to be punished.

Hopefully the punishment will help you to learn that you must care about the things around you.

If you *choose* to be destructive, you may need to be punished.

Hopefully the punishment will help you to learn that you should not be destructive on purpose.

When you are destructive, you often hurt yourself as well as the people around you. Thus, you should try not to be destructive.